THE ENGINEERS

KATY LEDERER

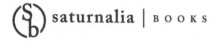

saturnalia | BOOKS

Distributed by Independent Publishers Group
Chicago

Saturnalia Books
105 Woodside Rd.
Ardmore, PA 19003
info@saturnaliabooks.com

ISBN: 978-1-947817-60-9 (print), 978-1-947817-61-6 (ebook)
Library of Congress Control Number: 2023933348

Cover art and Book design by Robin Vuchnich

Distributed by:
Independent Publishing Group
814 N. Franklin St.
Chicago, IL 60610
800-888-4741

CONTENTS

FETUS PAPYRACEUS   3

INFLAMMATION   5

VANISHING TWIN   10

AUTOPHAGY   12

POLAR BODIES   13

TRANSLOCATIONS   23

HISTOLOGY   24

CROWNING   27

SIMILE   32

MASS EFFECT   42

CHIMERAS   43

ATTENTION DEFICIT   45

FROZEN ANGELS   47

ECTOPIC   49

TUBES   50

MUTATIONS I   52

MUTATIONS II   53

MUTATIONS III   59

ORGANISMS   60

NEGATIVE CAPABILITY   61

BLOODY SHOW   66

LOVE   67

PARTURITION   69

AUTOIMMUNITY   71

ACEPHALIC   72

PHANTOM TWIN   74

Notes   76
Citations   79
Acknowledgments   81
About the Author   83

FETUS PAPYRACEUS

Sometimes, in the middle
of the night, our children will
insist that we tell them a story.
In the story, after heavy
rhyme and insistent inculcation
of our customary ways,
our children will look down
at our apparent missing limbs,
which remind them
that they should not touch,
and, if they do decide to touch,
that absence will feel presence.
It can be difficult, this lesson,
and the children are defenseless
as we read to them this book.
They like to flap their hands
and look: at animals that long ago
died out. They roar and raise
their trunks. They lurk, alertly,
in their dens. We wonder
what has happened to their spirits
and discover, as an exercise,

such thinking is instructive.
Where is the presence
and the absence in this book?
The world is full of lulls
and shocks. To describe them all
would take a million lives.
What would it mean
to use up our one life like this?
And so we peel the pages back.
It is a treasure, this book.
It is a treasure beyond
the other treasures in the world,
because the book is like
nothing. It is blank
with little colors there.
Made from deciduous forest
and the end of time. We had once
walked along the boardwalks
very bored, in heavy weather,
under moonlit stars.
We had once held
our children in our arms.

INFLAMMATION

1.
We had been short-term, irresponsible.
How we had lived inside a house.

How we had lived inside a hole.
Dolor (pain), *calor* (heat), *rubor* (redness), *tumor* (swelling),
　　　functio laesa (loss of function).

We can look into the tissue,
can examine the fine gradient.

We can speak in foreign languages, the language of the internet,
or maybe in the language of cell death.

Have we reached the site of injury?
We have been injurious.

Have we served well on our jury?
We have juried. We have *jured* and *jured*.

We are sad.
Sad as a parent.

How then is the weather right outside?
We see the sunlight. It is raw out on the landscape, where we try
　　　to hide.

We miss the internet.
It let us search.

We searched for our lost children,
but on the same day that we found them, we abandoned them.

2.
We write.
We write of phagocytes.

We write of chemokines.
We write.

We write of fibrin clots, coagulation systems.
We are missing our three ghosts.

The vasoactive host.
The mother is the host.

The mast cells as the chemoattractant.
Let us take our chemotaxi to the moon.

The moon is like a heaven or a mother or an open wound.
Our children once manifested themselves as swelling.

We are contemplating children,
the attack phase of immune.

3.

How we like it when the words collide.
In rhyme, to make a parallel.

Metonymy: we like it well enough.
One child, two child, three.

Put them all with one another in a dish and you get
triplets.

Metaphor: we like it well enough.
One child, two child, three.

The same person, just
"one and the same."

How we talk to ourselves,
like a parent.

Simile is best, the more specific:
how we like our one, we like our two, we like our three.

One is like two is like three.
We like our simile.

It may be that plasma-derived proteins allow these enzymes to act
as inflammatory mediators.
Is this real life?

4.
We break down.
Instead of grandpa we call the man granule.

Instead of sibling we write histamine.
We swell and we swell in an arteriole dilation that increases venous
permeability.

Adherence, chemotaxis.
We get into our taxis.

Racing around the genetic lottery universe,
wailing.

We love to say granulosa cells:
sounds like sugar.

Purulent:
disgusting, like it sounds, that filled with pus.

Serous: sounds like serious.
With serous, you get copious, nonviscous, and skin blisters.

Ulcerous: sounds serious.
Remove the dermal layer, hurt.

Thrombotic complications: how our hearts will thromb and thromb
          and thromb.
(That makes three thrombs.)

They thromb for children
that could be.

This is the side effect of being we.
The reproduction of our we.

VANISHING TWIN

We were a dynasty
of symmetry.
Whenever we expected
that the screen would inflect
with our image—one face,
two face—
we would have to turn
our heads, concerned
we could
not see, or would

not want to see
the double truth. The fee
would be exorbitant
no matter how unconfident
the doctor might have been
in what he'd seen.
O holy writ
of God. Before we sit
down to be told
we are old,

before we stand up,
or get back in the stirrups,
we pray: please let us know
what makes one grow,
the other shrink
against the back-
ground, black and white,
like snow at night,
or stars descending
then vanishing.

AUTOPHAGY

Flotsam from the world we were, and dirty.
The cells would malfunction. We'd suffer from a medical mystery.

Waste would accumulate nightly. We'd rest.
The two of us were energy. We'd measure the effect.

The findings were exciting.
Weeks of running, we would diet.

When not resting, we'd suffer severe psychological stress.
We would exercise, of course, and stretch.

We moved throughout the camps as if the agent of the chaperone.
Otherwise, we surely would have perished in the lysosome.

When the membranes that engulf debris inside the cells would glow,
we would let go. Each day we spent living. Mitochondria burned.

POLAR BODIES

We were polar
and bipedal.
From our helmets
flowed
genetic hair.
Prepared to fare
the structures—cool
dense regions, closed
concentric fields—
we lucked
our way
from shield
to shield, one body
to the other.

*

Believing we
were one of them,
we had been
oiled, we had been
sunned.
Believing that
the day was done,
the moon arcing over the ocean.
Before we took
our temperatures,
our bodies would be
covered in scald
scales and soft
incendiary furs.

*

Our bodies piled
in rows
in snow:
we carried to the active zone
the ones
we had known best.
Once warned,
our faces would be
shorn, our enemies
would be
informed,
but how the sunlight
shone upon
our mutilated wrists.

*

We were
wave heating,
but we hated them.
The plasmas
that were
lost in space
were captured
in the cold.
We had been sold
before the aircraft
rolled, our bodies
bridled, bodies
brined by beautiful
coronas.

*

First one, then two
coronal loops,
we bodied through,
ambiguous.
The statues
smashed,
the crescents
pushed,
the laboratory
nano-flares
beneath the burning
bush. And then
we felt their
soothing touch.

*

O cool magnetic
force. O
cloud gas. O
uncontrolled and
equilibrious
lost regions.
At once in situ
in our sitting place,
we acquiesced
into a state.
But still the State
decided that our bodies
had to be
contained.

*

We had been spectral
in our particles.
In a white zodiacal light
we found
our bodies had been
braised,
our faces faded
by a brazen wind.
Before we could begin
to know what happened,
we would have to send
a flare
of observation
to the moon.

*

Magnetic in our magnitude,
we influenced
our captors to release
the choking sphere.
If we had lived
in fear, we didn't now.
Our comrades hid
behind the cloud.
Could we let go?
We asked until our
bodies burst,
our ankles pin–
wheeled into outer
space.

*

We did not know
which way to run,
and so
we wandered
toward the sun, protected
by a psalter.
Our bodied heads un-
helmeted, our
scars and stitches
in our hands,
we hardened and we—
hardening—
lay down in the
dark dell.

*

It was a wretched
place and we
were also wretched,
quadrupolar sun
and tangled helmet
streamers in our hair.
O village, what's your
warning flare?
You did not
dare. You did
not dare. And now
we're here, our
bodies reconfigured,
into bells.

TRANSLOCATIONS

We de-notate and detonate. At breakpoint, we will close our eyes.
We replicate abnormally. We suffer from the rational.
We radiate excessively, fold into flats then flex our thighs.
We cycle then proliferate. We implicate, psychologize.

We replicate abnormally. We suffer from the rational.
Both balanced and unbalanced, we will call ourselves reciprocal.
We cycle then proliferate. We implicate, psychologize.
Our eyes will form before the splice. Our brains will not be typical.

Both balanced and unbalanced, we will call ourselves reciprocal.
Our arms are short. Our legs are long. Our sex will be consensual.
Our eyes will form before the splice. Our brains will not be typical:
Both fibrate and synovial, homologous and cauterized.

Our arms are short. Our legs are long. Our sex will be consensual.
We radiate excessively, fold into flats then flex our thighs:
Both fibrate and synovial, homologous and cauterized.
We de-notate and detonate. At breakpoint, we will close our eyes.

HISTOLOGY

Embedding media, we prayed.

—

Immiscibility. Epoxy. God.

—

Unmolten, only histamine. In soft acrylic resin.

—

We might grow talons in this ethanol, or talents. Might grow ethical.

—

Peripheral as tumors we were bled.

—

With formalin we had been formed.

—

Ablutions and ablations, born.

—

We knew we would be hybridized. We lyricized our God.

———

God as fixation and as fixative, as figural cremation. The man who never was.
        The great un-mother. Manometer.

———

We had to exit through this artifact.

———

We had been trying like a sibling to be born.

———

We were not born.

———

———

Perpendicular to each other, we personified amorphousness, delinquency of life, a soulful jackknife, plunging into hearts and bloodying our heads, a lethal forceps.

CROWNING

We wore a
garland wreath,
but it was

tight around
our necks. We
spun around,

we took our
trousers down,
admired the

searing brands
that now our
buttocks did

adorn. (Our
torsos and
our limbs were

shorn.) Instead
of bone, they
fed us fat.

Instead of
coffee, crème
brûlée. And

what a meal
our captors
made! Before,

the sinew
like a floss,
but now we

were gourmet,
ensauced. We
like to speak

about it
with tined and
tasty tongues.

While we were
mauled when some-
one dropped the

tongs, we knew
we would soon
be devoured,

be part of
a real meal.
We had been

hungry, we
had been in
thrall. But now

we would not
have to won-
der when or

where the light
might shine from
there, behind

our heads. Or
where upon
the esplan-

ade we would
have to crouch
down in a

terrified
ball. No, we
would have to

wonder not
at all. In
winter, sum-

mer, spring, or
fall. We would
be free to

crawl into
a safe, a-
waiting mouth.

The mouth would
welcome us.
The mouth would

be just like
a garland
wreath, a wreath

with teeth. The
pleasure of
the mouth that

took us in
would be the
pleasure of

our crowning.
The reverse
of birth. An

intake of
the uni-
verse, unburst.

SIMILE

Like
metaphor: two components brought together.

Egg: coin
Sperm: sun

We pay shade money
for this son.

Egg: mountain
Sperm: universe

Diverse,
the largeness of our hurt.

Egg: wood
Sperm: would

A pun,
a pun baby.

Egg: tears
Sperm: rain

A simile as
baby

like
a baby,

sun and simile,
dried up.

*

We like
to smile and simile.

Red, just
that rosaceous

quick
and quickened.

Quick is just
a word for life.

Quicken like
clay thickening

toward some dark, hardened
way of life.

What if we just
made statues? Just

that cooling and that
thickening?

Here we are in culture.
Cinched, injected,

rescued,
rescuing.

*

Never fields of study, only
knowledge growing on the vine.

Egg: accrual
Sperm: grapes

We ape and ape,
then drink our wine.

Egg: never
Sperm: shape

One is entered,
one will enter, fine.

Egg: martyr
Sperm: martyr

Refused
to take another form.

Egg: confusion
Sperm: order

We have been ordering our children,
we have ordered them to pause.

We like to hold them
in our jaws.

*

We release the lonely women from their tears,
we tear their hearts and ears

like
a terror.

Our trained physicians will release us now,
the children like

the hounds of hell, pursuing us
relentlessly from bed.

*

Egg: fir
Sperm: snow

Settling,
it is beautiful.

Egg: box
Sperm: bow

Tied up
like

the present,
or tubes.

*

The children parse us.
The children make us

as their marks. They do it
with their eyes shut tight, like

magic.
Hands bent, heads loose like

bowling balls.
Never could the sample then

require...what?
Something...happiness?

Something like
a happiness or sadness.

*

There on the table,
spread eagle.

Never again will we lie.
But we lie.

Egg: happenstance
Sperm: happenstance

Never again will we cry.
But we cry similarly.

MASS EFFECT

Pushed together, pulled apart, we were purported pluripotent.
We developed as an organ, a benign and beating heart.
We looked up doctors for ontology. Discovered spinal symmetry.
Within the sacred bowl of life, our innards spilled in red array.

I wondered what you'd have to say if in your mouth you grew a tongue.
I wondered what I'd have to say if in my face I grew a mouth.
Instead, we moved into a house, connected by a modem.
A surgical removal could have cured us of our malady,

but seeking to remain benign, we discoursed through telepathy.
How long could we have lived like this?
With our then-rudimentary eyes, we saw shapes coming toward us:
amorphous and black, shedding tears. We had nothing to say.

CHIMERAS

Thyroid, thyroid, what do you see?
I see a hydrops looking at me.

Hydrops, hydrops, what do you see?
I see an amnion looking at me.

Amnion, amnion, what do you see?
I see an organelle looking at me.

Organelle, organelle, what do you see?
I see a tumor looking at me.

Tumor, tumor, what do you see?
I see a disomy looking at me.

Disomy, disomy, what do you see?
I see a vesicle looking at me.

Vesicle, vesicle, what do you see?
I see an X-ray looking at me.

X-ray, X-ray, what do you see?
I see a carrier looking at me.

Carrier, carrier, what do you see?
I see a poetess looking at me.

Poetess, poetess, what do you see?
I see a reader looking at me.

Reader, reader, what do you see?
I see:
A thyroid
A hydrops
An amnion
An organelle
A tumor
A disomy
A vesicle
An X-ray
And a carrier.
That's what I see.

ATTENTION DEFICIT

Focus for
us was a thing hard to
come by. We would have to make do with
whatever

we had: these
were pills and a pencil,
blue earplugs to block out the voices
inside of

our heads, which
would tell us time passed and
these thoughts that would shine like soft lights on
our brains, would

one day fade
into invisible
relief. We would write in our binders,
pass classes,

allow for
a moment of grief. We
were deeply aware we would have to
make up for

lost time, but
when we took our pills, the
world would seem fine, seem as if it had
always been

fine. Once we
had adequate supplies
we'd sell, but until then we decid-
ed to re-

fill. We had
determined that we would
not brood. Instead we charted out our
moods and light-

ened up our
loads. Before the rest of
time unfolds, we would like to hold on-
to this life,

feel like it's
beating, there, deep inside
of our chests, not out of fear. We are
just children.

FROZEN ANGELS

Viable 1

Could we be beautiful?
Unbeautiful.

Be fruitful.
We are fruitful.

Be truthful:
we feel nothing. We are as hopeful

as a dormant spring. Would it be sorrowful
to be unborn? As literal as anything, as artful

as we go to womb. The world will be as bountiful
without us and as beautiful.

Viable 2

We were lonely
and we wondered

if we might have been the only
ones. Considered

dearly
othered,

we were drearily
here kept. We weathered

weather while we slept. Professionally
here stored.

Viable 3

Human ardor produced
us. We were forced

from non-existence, loosed
then fettered.

At first we had been blessed,
but we were buried

as we slept. We had been mothered
then unmothered;

composed
then unconceived.

ECTOPIC

Within us teeth, and hair, and skin.
We climbed the snowy mountain then discovered that we had no shins.
Unable to continue, we harangued ourselves in parkas.
Unlike the others, who had been poised, we were not ready to escape.

If re-absorbed, we could have cut the rope.
If we had hemorrhaged, we could block. We could not talk.
Without concern at our conception that the alloy would abate,
we were delinquent, lost a lot of weight.

Congenital, nocturnal, in our cystic diagnosis, we decided we would stay the night.
We undid our skull sutures like hats.
We lay down on our sides on our mats and reclined.
We were late, and excruciatingly hungry.

TUBES

Mesosalpinx   Salpinx   Hydrosalpinx

Hematosalpinx   Asalpinx (nothing)

Besalpinx

Desalpinx

Acanthosalpinx

Paucisalpinx

Intersalpinx   Intrasalpinx

Lacrimosalpinx (sad)

Obsalpinx

Anisosalpinx

Atelosalpinx   Schizosalpinx (two or double)

Brachysalpinx

Ceratosalpinx   Cyanosalpinx

Isosalpinx (metaphor, simile)

                                    Phagosalpinx

Panosalpinx

Metrosalpinx

                                    Pleiosalpinx

Pterygosalpinx (taking wing)

MUTATIONS I

We had been organisms mostly, as we slung our legs across the plain.
Observed, we were observable. Before we saw, we closed our eyes.
Before we could become ourselves, we had to name the animals:
successive in our shortening, unable to extend our lives.

Observed, we were observable. Before we knocked, we closed our eyes.
Late-acting, deleterious, we saw by death we would be had.
Successful in our shortening, unable to extend our lives.
Contemplative without our tails, we knew we'd say what could be said.

Lactating, deleterious, we saw by death we would be had.
What seeking unobtainable, pursuing prey, we closed right in.
Contemplative without our tales, we knew we'd say what could be said.
What knowing was unknowable, without our eyes we might have seen.

What seeking inexplicable, pursuing prey, we closed right in.
Before we could control ourselves, we had to name the animals.
What showing was un-showable, without our eyes we might have seen.
As organisms mostly, we would sling our lives across the pain.

MUTATIONS II

We had been organisms mostly, as we slung our legs across the plain.
Not missing in the opening.
Or laughing.
We had lost our tongues.

Not missing in the opening,
we wanted to believe.
But with our tongues
we could not speak.

We had been captured then released.
We had once lived in the high foliage—sky a terminating crèche.
We had not spoken.
You had wanted to believe us.

In the fuselage we lived, the sky a crash.
We would not laugh.
But you believed us.
We were organisms mostly.

*

We had been organisms mostly, as we slung our legs across the plain.
Not missing opportunity,
collapsing,
we had lost our way.

Not missing in monotony,
we knew we could not sing.
Within our mouths,
we could not sing.

We had been captured in the breach,
we had to settle. We were prone to search.
Unable to be saved,
we had no church.

Before the search,
collapsible.
We knew we had no church,
but prone to searching, we were organisms mostly.

*

Organisms mostly.
We were open in the closest sense.
Once keepers,
we were prone to loss.

That open,
in our opulence, we had to prove the rule,
which had been loss.
We put him on the cross.

We had to prove the rule
that truly we were family.
As we put him on the cross,
the mother howled.

As we put him on the cross,
we had been keepers in the loosest sense.
Thus hallowed,
we were organisms mostly.

*

We had been organisms mostly,
had been banished from the task.
But with our intellects
we learned to ask.

We had been banished from the task,
but we could ask.
We had to think
outside of instinct.

We had to ask,
though first we had to crutch.
We lurched
to get to church.

We were on crutches
in the church.
We used our intellects.
We slung our legs.

*

We had been organisms mostly.
We were lying, but no longer maned.
With motive,
we became the same.

Some had to crawl,
some had to push.
A range of new emotions
made us renovate and rush.

But we had changed.
We roamed a wider range.
Now rushing
we would learn to rage.

We had to roam a wider range,
array our motivations,
walk the solitary stage.
Our legs were slung. Still organisms mostly.

*

We had been organisms mostly, as we slung our legs across the plain.
Not slouching in the opening.
Or arching.
We would use our thumbs.

Not slouching in the opening,
we wanted to believe.
And with our brains
we could believe.

We hadn't mattered in the trees.
We had once lived in the high foliage—sky a blue and baffling reach.
We had not spoken.
Tongue intransigent.

In the futile age we lived, the sky was cash.
We studied math.
Now we were organisms mostly.
We believed us.

MUTATIONS III

We had been organisms talking.
What to say. What not to say.
The world a roiling, rolling day.
We did not know what we could say.

We could not hate
without our faith.
We killed our meat and made our tools.
We swam in chlorinated pools.

We learned to think and talk.
We became cruel and very frightened.
We knew that one day we would die.
No one knew why.

ORGANISMS

Organism   Enzyme   Myeloid
Oncogene   Centromere   Toxic
Xylem   Extrinsic
Pleiotropic

Organism   Zygote   Gonad
Origin   Osmotic   Tracheids
Axis   Mitotic
Mutagenic

Organism   Diploid   Soma
Blastula   Fibroblast   Basal
Taxa   Radical
Meiosis

Organism   Proxy   Lifespan
Optimum   Stilbenoid   Spindle
Neuron   Surgeon
Lymphoma

Organism   Golgi   Lethal
Depleted   Replicative   Healthspan
Histone   Hapten
Stochastic

NEGATIVE CAPABILITY

Under decree.
Lasts approximately

continuously. Departs
from the pre-

ovulatory, folliculating
process.

We underwent
procedures. In

the glass we put
the trophoblast.

*

Fully formed antrum.
Presence of

a class two cell.
Fully formed in

estrogen. Pre-
ovulation stage.

Cortex post-
conception,

in the follicle.
Decrease the range.

*

We had been
basal lamina,

surrounded by
a beveled back.

The presence of
the theca

cells, the small
and slack

mitotic cells,
primordial

and sacked.
We made

our embryos
to order.

*

We were in transition
region. Hands on

legs, our ankles
overdone.

Between the blanks
aromified,

renewal calculation
as a cowl or caul

or catacomb.
The trophoblast

now in
its tube.

*

Human proved
mechanical.

The mother's egg,
X chromosome.

In the absence of
fertilization, the egg

eventually
traversed. In distal of

the ostia,
the humans

we would recognize
as us.

BLOODY SHOW

Here, a shroud or shred.
Something bony. A hand,

here, or a wing, splayed
out. Subsequently, our

condition was discovered
to be a fetus. Our lives

were then discovered to be
fetuses. Everything was

a fetus, but then nothing
was a fetus, and our eyes

broke into guarded life.

LOVE

We wanted to believe in something powerful and true, like love.
We wanted to believe in love.
We wanted to believe in something powerful and true.

And so we raised our heads above.
And so we were a me and you.
We wanted to believe in something powerful and true, like love.

And when the push had come to shove.
We had to work to make it through.
We wanted to believe in love.

We didn't wear our socks or gloves,
our toes and fingers turning blue.
We wanted to believe in something powerful and true, like love.

Until we could be rid of
pain. Until the others got their due,
we wanted to believe in love.

It was of
truth, by truth, we were seduced.
We wanted to believe in something powerful and true, like love.
We wanted to believe in love.

We wanted to believe in something powerful and true, like love.
We wanted to believe in love.
We wanted to believe in something powerful and true.

PARTURITION

Birth as decreased
umbilical function.
Layer upon layer.

Available figuration
for unavailable creation.
Birth as a fantasy of loss.

Ovarian in mantle
like a fighter, hands
come out fanning.

We reach out with our
fingers: nothing there.
We try to splay

our wings, but we
can feel it is impossible.
There is this relevance,

irrelevance. Emotional
to speak in sterile language,
unemotional.

We dreamed
our hands could splay,
our wings could spread.

As trophoblast,
we could not latch.
This must be sadness.

AUTOIMMUNITY

Our tolerance was evident.
Proposed since birth, since origin.

The antigen or pathogen.
The pathogen contagion.

When pathos might prevent the young result.
We are now running from the steroid and the postulate perception:

the idiotype, how to call it?
We called it lymphocyte, which self-reacts.

I loathe it mostly and react.
We had, according to our needs,

then reached plateau,
but antigens were absent still.

ACEPHALIC

In a pulse of light, we saw him.
Standing with his back to the wind.
His brain, there, sopping in his hands:
"God." What does it mean, the two small
eyes, now going empty, and the hole,
there, in his missing chin? Our God.

"God," we like to say. The word
a holder, like his hands. We want
to hold our God. In name.

He was the manipulator of light.
Not with his hands, but with his
brain. Put two words together. Call it
juxtaposition. In the conference
presentation, he went sane. He
threw up both his hands and brain.

"God," we like to say. The word
a holder, like his hands. We want
to hold our God. In name.

We mourn our neurons. Turning on
and off. We see our switches in his hands.
We want our breath, our brains, our
thought. What if our brains were in
our hands? No breath, no thought, but still
we would be able to destroy the world.

PHANTOM TWIN

We did not want to be
unblessed, so we were
blessed. High, thin wire,

a little ground where
we might lay our heads.
It was this way, this looking

fore and back, a pole held
tightly in our hands. You
want to tell me what went

wrong? Contumely shapes
across a wall, depression in
the ground. The gorgeous

soldiers fought and fell. *Hie
unto hell.* How we will lie
in that brave grave apart,

our aperture: a heart
that has been ruptured
absolutely by a passing god.

NOTES

"Fetus Papyraceus": Sometimes during a twin pregnancy, one twin dies and eventually becomes flattened—like paper—inside the womb.

"Vanishing Twin": A vanishing twin is a twin that dies in the womb and is eventually absorbed into the mother or the other twin.

"Autophagy": composed of the Greek *auto*, which means "self" and *phagy*, which means "to eat." A metabolic process by which the body cleans out old, damaged, or dysfunctional cell parts by "eating" itself.

"Polar Bodies": In reproductive discourse, a polar body is a cell given off by an oocyte, or egg, during meiosis. In reproductive engineering, these polar bodies can be biopsied and tested for genetic abnormalities.

"Translocations": Chromosomal translocation is when all or part of a chromosome becomes attached to or interchanged with another chromosome or part thereof. Chromosomal translocations can be "balanced," which means there is no net gain or loss of chromosomal material, and, in some cases, no dysfunction, or "unbalanced," which means a loss or gain of chromosomal material results in a defect or dysfunction. Chromosomal translocations can cause miscarriage and post-birth complications and suffering.

"Histology" is the study of the microanatomy of tissues, typically requiring that samples be sectioned (cut into thin slices) and stained. This poem is mimetic in that it is sectioned and, in some poetic sense, stained.

"Chimeras": In reproductive discourse, a chimera is an organism composed of genetically distinct cells. In humans, one cell line usually becomes dominant, therefore obscuring the existence of the other cell line. Sometimes, however, chimerism can result in an organism with two different eye colors, uneven or patchy hair or skin color, and other visually mismatched phenotypes. In Greek mythology, the Chimera was a fire-breathing creature with a lion's head, a goat's body, and a serpent's head or tail. This poem's form is taken from the ubiquitous children's book *Brown Bear, Brown Bear, What Do You See?* by Bill Martin Jr. and Eric Carle.

"Tubes": The common word *tube*, as in "fallopian tube," comes down to us from the Latin *tuba*. A few very specialized medical terms take a different instrument—the Greek *salpinx*, which was more like a trumpet—as the root to denote a tubal structure. "Mesosalpinx" is the tissue that encloses the ovary (like a blanket or curtain, in my imagination). "Hydrosalpinx" is a condition in which the fallopian tube is blocked by fluid. I found this root of interest—strange, in some way humorous. I added meaningful prefixes to it to create the half-poetic, half-medical-sounding variants in this poem.

"Acephalic" means literally "without a head" and can describe a fetus that does not develop a head. In some twin pregnancies, a headless fetus may become attached at the neck to the headed twin, thereby becoming parasitic. Georges Bataille also used this term to evoke a headless or godless social order, a model of anarchy.

"Phantom twin" is another way of denoting a "vanishing twin." I think the use of "phantom" in this phrasing more strongly implies that the living twin might sense the ghostly presence of the absent twin.

CITATIONS

It would not be possible for me to credit every single article, blog entry, listserv, Wikipedia entry, or informational website that inspired these poems, and from which words, phrases, and concepts were reproduced. Some of the more moving, troubling, and surprising pieces I came across included the following:

From Wikipedia: "Autoimmunity"; "Autophagy"; "Chimera (genetics)"; "Chromosomal translocations"; "Corona"; "Follicular Atresia"; "Histology"; "Immunodeficiency"; "Inflammation"; "Mosaics (genetics)"; "Senescence"; "Telomere"; and "Teratoma."

From the *New York Times* and *New York Times Magazine*: Rachel E. Gross, "Ovaries Are Prone to 'Exhaustion' and 'Fatigue.' Or Are They?" March 29, 2022; Donald G. McNeil Jr., "A Twin Inside a Twin: In Colombia, an Extraordinary Birth," March 20, 2019; Tamar Lewin, "Babies from Skin Cells?: Prospect Is Unsettling to Some Experts," May 16, 2017; Andrew Pollack, "Scientists Add Letters to DNA's Alphabet, Raising Hope and Fear," May 7, 2014; Carl Zimmer, "Young Blood May Hold Key to Reversing Aging," May 4, 2014; Carl Zimmer, "Seeing X Chromosomes in a New Light," January 20, 2014; Gina Kolata, "Autism's Unexpected Link to Cancer Genes," August 11, 2013; Gina Kolata, "Alzheimer's Tied to Mutation Harming Immune Response," November 14, 2012; Gina Kolata, "How Do You Live Knowing You Might Have an Alzheimer's Gene?" June 7, 2012; Benedict Carey, "Scientists Link Gene Mutation to Autism Risk," April 4, 2012; Gretchen Reynolds, "Exercise as Housecleaning for the Body," February 1, 2012; L. Alan Sroufe, "Ritalin Gone Wrong," January 28, 2012; and Gardiner Harris, "F.D.A. Finds Short Supply of Attention Deficit Drugs," December 31, 2011.

The following videos and films: "Scientists Grow Lamb Fetus Inside Artificial Womb," *Insider Tech* YouTube channel, April 26, 2017; "The 46 Year Pregnancy" (documentary), from the series *Extraordinary People*, original airdate March 27, 2006; and *Frozen Angels* (documentary), directed by Eric Black and Frauke Sandig, 2005.

Other sources: Ethan Bronner and Chen Shalita, "Postmortem Sperm Retrieval Is Turning Dead Men Into Fathers," *Bloomberg Businessweek*, July 19, 2022; "Sacrococcygeal Teratoma (SCT)," Center for Fetal Diagnosis and Treatment at the Children's Hospital of Philadelphia, March 2014; Mark Johnston, "Is Life a Ponzi Scheme?" *Boston Review*, January 2, 2014; João Pedro de Magalhães, "Immortality and Society," Senescence.Info (blog), 2013 iteration; Reason, "Autophagy and Cellular Senescence," Fight Aging! (blog), May 21, 2009; and Joshua Johnson et al., "Germline Stem Cells and Follicular Renewal in the Postnatal Mammalian Ovary," *Nature*, March 11, 2004. I also owe a debt to Susan Wheeler's formally inventive and innovative book *Smokes* (Four Way Books, 1998), which served as a playful teacher as I wrote the first few poems in the collection; and also to Wittgenstein's brilliant final treatise, still unfinished when he passed away, *On Certainty*.

ACKNOWLEDGMENTS

The following poems first appeared, often as different versions, in:

6x6: "Negative Capability"
Academy of American Poets: "Attention Deficit," "Phantom Twin," "Mass Effect"
The American Poetry Review: "Acephalic," "Crowning," "Frozen Angels"
The Awl: "Fetus Papyraceus"
Bomb Cyclone: "Bloody Show," "Parturition"
Boston Review's "What Nature" *online forum*: "Polar Bodies"
The Colorado Review: "Inflammation"
CURA: "Simile"
EDNA: The Magazine of the Millay Colony for the Arts: "Translocations"
FOU: "Mutations I," "Mutations II," "Mutations III," "Organisms"
The Literary Review: "Love"
The Iowa Review: "Autophagy"
VOLT: "Histology"

Thanks to: Michael Slosek and Katie Klocksin for featuring "Phantom Twin" on the Poetry Foundation's *PoetryNow* podcast (2019); Rob Mc-Lennan at above/ground press for producing the chapbook, *The Children* (2017), which includes several of these poems; Joe Pan and Jason Koo at Brooklyn Arts Press for including "Translocations" and "Autophagy" in their *Brooklyn Poets Anthology* (2017); and Erin Belieu for choosing a section of this series as runner-up for the Poetry Society of America's Fay Di Castignola Award for a manuscript in progress.

"Negative Capability" was composed in response to a prompt, "twins," I was given for the Double Take reading series in New York; thanks to Jennifer Firestone for asking me to partner with her on this prompt.

Gratitude also to MacDowell for hosting me at a residency as I worked on many of the poems in the book.

ABOUT THE AUTHOR

Katy Lederer is the author of three previous books of poetry and a memoir. Her poems, essays, reported features, and reviews have appeared online and in print in the *American Poetry Review*, *n+1*, the *New York Times*, the *New Yorker*, and the *Paris Review*, among many other publications. She has taught poetry workshops and climate change writing at Columbia University, Fordham University, Barnard College, and the New School.

Also by Katy Lederer

Poetry

Winter Sex
The Heaven-Sent Leaf
The bright red horse—and the blue—

Memoir

Poker Face: A Girlhood Among Gamblers

The Engineers is printed in Adobe Caslon Pro.
www.saturnaliabooks.org